Spontaneity
(Numbers 22, Matthew 17, Acts 20)

Spontaneity sparks a smile,
Massages out conflicts' kinks,
Freshens routine relationships,
And just might tickle a laboring lover
Turning blue beneath a tourniquet
Of bellowing bills and clingy calls.
Breaking patterns helps, too.
Ha! I caught you looking
When I alleviated alliteration.
Now send a smile somewhere sour.

ALSO BY SHARON OLDS

Satan Says
The Dead and the Living
The Gold Cell

The Father

The Father

by
Sharon Olds

Alfred A. Knopf   New York   1994

THIS IS A BORZOI BOOK
PUBLISHED BY ALFRED A. KNOPF, INC.

"The Race," "The Lumens," and "The Feelings" originally appeared
in *The New Yorker*.

Other poems in this work were originally published in the following
publications: *The Agni Review*, *The American Poetry Review*,
Antaeus, *Bastard Review*, *Chelsea*, *Field*, *The Gettysburg Review*,
Heresies, *Indiana Review*, *The Iowa Review*, *Iron* (Great Britain),
The Paris Review, *Poetry*, *Poetry East*, *The Quarterly*, *Salmagundi*,
Slow Dancer (Great Britain), *The Threepenny Review*.

Library of Congress Cataloging-in-Publication Data

Olds, Sharon.
    The father / by Sharon Olds. — 1st ed.
       p.   cm.
  PS3565.L34F38   1992
  811'.54–dc20   91–35719
                                               CIP

Manufactured in the United States of America
Published May 1, 1992
Reprinted Twice
Fourth Printing, January 1994

Thanks to Galway Kinnell

sine quo
non hic liber

For my father

Contents

The Father

The Waiting

No matter how early I would get up
and come out of the guest room, and look down the hall,
there between the wings of the wing-back chair
my father would be sitting, his head calm
and dark between the wings. He sat
unmoving, like something someone has made,
his robe fallen away from his knees,
he sat and stared at the swimming pool
in the dawn. By then, he knew he was dying,
he seemed to approach it as a job to be done
which he knew how to do. He got up early
for the graveyard shift. When he heard me coming down the
hall he would not turn—he had
a way of holding still to be looked at,
as if a piece of sculpture could sense
the gaze which was running over it—
he would wait with that burnished, looked-at look until
the hem of my nightgown came into view,
then slew his eyes up at me, without
moving his head, and wait, the kiss
came to him, he did not go to it.
Now he would have some company
as he tried to swallow an eighth of a teaspoon
of coffee, he would have his child to give him
the cup to spit into, his child to empty it—
I would be there all day, watch him nap,
be there when he woke, sit with him
until the day ended, and he could get back into
bed with his wife. Not until the next
dawn would he be alone again, night-

watchman of matter, sitting, facing
the water—the earth without form, and void,
darkness upon the face of it, as if
waiting for his daughter.

Nullipara

The last morning of my visit, we sit
in our bathrobes, cronies, we cross and re-cross
our legs. Suddenly, he sees a thread
dangling from the cuff of my nightie, he cries out
Stay there! and goes to his desk drawer.
I hold my wrist out to him
and he stares with rigid concentration,
his irises balls of impacted matter.
He opens the shears, weighty and silvery-
brassy, the color of taint, he gets the
blades on either side of the thread
close to the cuff—he wants to get it
exactly right, to do me a service
at the end of his life. He snips once
and we sigh, we get fresh coffee and feel it
enter us. He knows he will live in me
after he is dead, I will carry him like a mother.
I do not know if I will ever deliver.

The Pulling

Every hour, now, he is changing,
shedding some old ability.
Knees up, body tin-colored,
hair black and grey, thick with
grease like ritual unguent, my father
moves, hour by hour, head-first,
toward death, I sense every inch of him moving
through me toward it, the way each child
moved, slowly, down through my body,
as if I were God feeling the rivers
pulling steadily through me, and the earth
pressing through, the universe
itself hauled through me heavily and easily,
drawn through my body like a napkin through a ring—
as if my father could live and die
safely inside me.

The Glass

I think of it with wonder now,
the glass of mucus that stood on the table
in front of my father all weekend. The tumor
is growing fast in his throat these days,
and as it grows it sends out pus
like the sun sending out flares, those pouring
tongues. So my father has to gargle, cough,
spit a mouthful of thick stuff
into the glass every ten minutes or so,
scraping the rim up his lower lip
to get the last bit off his skin, then he
sets the glass down on the table and it
sits there, like a glass of beer foam,
shiny and faintly golden, he gargles and
coughs and reaches for it again
and gets the heavy sputum out,
full of bubbles and moving around like yeast—
he is like a god producing food from his own mouth.
He himself can eat nothing anymore,
just a swallow of milk, sometimes,
cut with water, and even then
it can't always get past the tumor,
and the next time the saliva comes up
it is ropey, he has to roll it in his throat
a minute to form it and get it up and dis-
gorge the oval globule into the
glass of phlegm, which stood there all day and
filled slowly with compound globes and I would
empty it and it would fill again
and shimmer there on the table until
the room seemed to turn around it

in an orderly way, a model of the solar system
turning around the sun,
my father the old earth that used to
lie at the center of the universe, now
turning with the rest of us
around his death, bright glass of
spit on the table, these last mouthfuls.

Death and Morality

My father's dying is not evil.
It is not good and it is not evil,
it is out of the moral world altogether.
When the nurses empty his catheter bag,
pouring the pale, amber fluid
into the hospital measuring cup, it is
neither good nor bad, it is only
the body. Even his pain, when his face
contracts, and his mouth makes a sucking snap
when his jaws draw back
is not wicked, no one is doing it to him,
there is no guilt, and no shame,
there is only pleasure and pain. This
is the world where sex lives, the world
of the nerves, the world without church,
we kiss him in it, we stroke back his gummed
hair, his wife and I, one
on either side, we wipe the flow of
saliva like ivory clay from the side of his mouth.
His body feels us attending him
outside the world of the moral, as if
we are making love to him in the woods
and we hear, far away, in a field,
the distant hymns of a tent-meeting,
smaller than the smallest drops of green-black
woods dew on his body as we dip to touch him.

The Picture I Want

It is black and white, square, thickly
glossed like a snapshot from a Baby Brownie.
He is sitting up, on the long couch,
a large man gone small with cancer.
In the open neck of his sports shirt
you can see some of the larger lumps
pressing out at his throat and chest,
he is like a stocking stuffed with things.
His head is leaning over far to one side,
resting on the top of my head, and my head
is leaning on his shoulder, my face as near
to the primary tumor as a dozing baby's
lips to the mother's breast. The light
is harsh, the shadows sharp, you can see
the lines of age on both our faces
and our eyes are closed—we are resting on each other,
almost asleep.

The Lumens

He is better, he is dying a little more slowly,
his skin gleams like wet silver,
he tilts his face up to me and it
flushes faintly rose, like a tray
reflecting the flowers it holds. They have drained
the blood out of his body and replaced it
with fresh blood from the people of Redwood City,
they have washed his hair and it lifts in a slow
wave above his brow. They shave him
and he glistens more, his skin is glossy,
he puts on his silver reading glasses and he
glitters, he lifts his eyelids and mild
sluices of shining come out of his eyes.
It is frightening to see how much light
this night man has had in him,
but we are not frightened. Luminous,
he sits up for minutes at a time and jokes,
we laugh, the nurses come in, and each
has a lumen around her folded cap, each
particle of air is capped with brightness
and he does not snuff it—before he dies,
my father dies as an extinguisher,
for minutes at a time he shines before he dies.

His Terror

He loves the portable altar the minister
brings to the hospital, its tiny cruets and
phials, its cross that stands up
when the lid opens, like the ballerina who un-
bent, when I opened my jewelry box, she
rose and twirled like the dead. Then the lid
folded her down, bowing, in the dark,
the way I would wait, under my bed,
for morning. My father has forgotten that,
he opens his mouth for the porous disc
to be laid on his tongue, he loves to call the minister *Father*.
And yet, somewhere in his body, is there terror?
The lumps of the cancer are everywhere now,
he can lay his palm where they swell his skin, he can
finger the holes where the surgeon has been in him.
He asks me to touch them.
Maybe his terror is not of dying,
or even of death, but of some cry
he has kept inside him all his life
and there are weeks left.

His Stillness

The doctor said to my father, "You asked me
to tell you when nothing more could be done.
That's what I'm telling you now." My father
sat quite still, as he always did,
especially not moving his eyes. I had thought
he would rave if he understood he would die,
wave his arms and cry out. He sat up,
thin, and clean, in his clean gown,
like a holy man. The doctor said,
"There are things we can do which might give you time,
but we cannot cure you." My father said,
"Thank you." And he sat, motionless, alone,
with the dignity of a foreign leader.
I sat beside him. This was my father.
He had known he was mortal. I had feared they would have
to tie him down. I had not remembered
he had always held still and kept silent to bear things,
the liquor a way to keep still. I had not
known him. My father had dignity. At the
end of his life his life began
to wake in me.

The Want

I waited down the hall, while his wife
settled my father down for the night,
adjusting the drip, wiping the dried
saliva out of the corners of his mouth,
making sure that the cup for the mucus
was near him, and the call button pinned to the sheet
like a pacifier tied to the bars of a crib.
I thought of the drip, the steel crank on the bed,
the call button, the cup, the light, I had
always known him as an object in the world
of objects because he would not speak,
sometimes, for a week,
but only make his signals—his fingers and
thumb stiffly opening and closing
like a beak: *Women yakking;* the heel of his
hand beating his forehead: *Women are so
stupid it destroys your mind.* I had stopped
longing for him to address me from his heart
before he died. I waited next to the
nurses' station, where the mothers leave
the bouquets when they take the baby home.
When she came out of his room she was shining—he had
taken her hands and thanked her for all
she had done for him for twenty years,
and then he had said *I want to devote
the rest of my life to you.*

The Lifting

Suddenly my father lifted up his nightie, I
turned my head away but he cried out
Shar!, my nickname, so I turned and looked.
He was sitting in the high cranked-up bed with the
gown up, around his neck,
to show me the weight he had lost. I looked
where his solid ruddy stomach had been
and I saw the skin fallen into loose
soft hairy rippled folds
lying in a pool of folds
down at the base of his abdomen,
the gaunt torso of a big man
who will die soon. Right away
I saw how much his hips are like mine,
the long, white angles, and then
how much his pelvis is shaped like my daughter's,
a chambered whelk-shell hollowed out,
I saw the folds of skin like something
poured, a thick batter, I saw
his rueful smile, the cast-up eyes as he
shows me his old body, he knows
I will be interested, he knows I will find him
appealing. If anyone had ever told me
I would sit by him and he would pull up his nightie
and I would look at him, at his naked body,
at the thick bud of his penis in all that
dark hair, look at him
in affection and uneasy wonder
I would not have believed it. But now I can still
see the tiny snowflakes, white and

night-blue, on the cotton of the gown as it
rises the way we were promised at death it would rise,
the veils would fall from our eyes, we would know everything.

The Look

When my father started choking again
he cried out *Back rub!* in a monotone,
as if making an announcement,
this man who had never asked me for anything.
He was too weak to lean forward much,
so I slid my hand between his hot
back and the hot sheet and he sat there
with his eyes bulging, those used India-
ink-eraser eyes that had never really
looked at me. His skin shocked me,
silky as a breast, voluptuous
as a baby's skin, but dry, and my hand
was dry, so I rubbed easily, in circles,
he stared and did not choke, I closed
my eyes and rubbed as if his body were his soul.
I could feel his backbone deep inside, I could
feel him under the rule of the choking,
all my life I had felt he was under a rule.
He gargled, I got the cup ready,
I didn't vary the stroke, he spat, I
praised him, I let the full pleasure
of caressing my father come awake in my body,
and then I could touch him from deep in my heart,
he shifted in the bed, he tilted, his eyes
bugged out and darkened, the mucus rose,
I held the cup to his lips and he slid out
the mass and sat back, a flush came into
his skin, and he lifted his head shyly but
without reluctance and looked at me
directly, for just a moment, with a dark
face and dark shining confiding eyes.

The Struggle

When the minister would come into the hospital room
my father would try to sit up, he would cry out
Up! Up! for us to raise his bed-head, then
silently he would wrestle himself
up, sweating, he would end up
leaning on the pillows, panting, a man, erect.
The minister would kiss him, they would pray, then chat,
he would hold his eyes open unblinking,
rigid adherent to the protocol of the living,
he would sit for the whole visit, and then,
the minute the man was out the door, cry
out *Down! Down!* and we would lower him
down, and he would pass out.
Later the doctor would pay a call and as
soon as my father saw that white coat
he would start to labor up, desperate
to honor the coat, at a glimpse of it he would
start to stir like a dog who could not
not obey. He would lurch, pause,
then thrust up slowly and unevenly, like a
camel, a half-born animal—the way,
they say, his soul will pull itself up
out of his dead body and wobblingly
walk. And then, one day, he tried,
his brain ordered his body to heave up,
the sweat rose in his pores but he was not
moving, he cast up his eyes as the minister
leaned to kiss him, he lay and stared, it was
nothing like the nights he had lain on the couch passed
out, nothing. Now he was alive,

awake, the raw boy of his heart stood
up each time a grown man
entered his death-room.

The Present Moment

Now that he cannot sit up,
now that he just lies there
looking at the wall, I forget the one
who sat up and put on his reading glasses
and the lights in the room multiplied in the lenses.
Once he entered the hospital
I forgot the man who lay full length
on the couch, with the blanket folded around him,
that huge, crushed bud, and I have
long forgotten the man who ate food—
not dense, earthen food, like liver, but
things like pineapple, wedges of light,
the skeiny nature of light made visible.
It's as if I abandoned that ruddy man
with the swollen puckered mouth of a sweet-eater,
the torso packed with extra matter
like a planet a handful of which weighs as much as the earth, I have
left behind forever that young man my father,
that smooth-skinned, dark-haired boy,
and my father long before I knew him, when he could
only sleep, or drink from a woman's
body, a baby who stared with a steady
gaze the way he lies there, now, with his
eyes open, then the lids start down
and the milky crescent of the other world
shines, in there, for a moment, before sleep.
I stay beside him, like someone in a rowboat
staying abreast of a Channel swimmer,
you are not allowed to touch them, their limbs
glow, faintly, in the night water.

Last Acts

I wish I could wash my father's face,
take cotton from the dirt of the earth
and run it over his face so the loops
lick in his pores before he dies. I want
to be in him, as I was once inside him,
riding in his balls the day before he cast me—
he carries me easily on his long legs up the
hills of San Francisco in war-time, I am
there between his legs where I belong,
I am his flesh, he can love me without
reserve, I will be his pleasure.
Now I want to feel, in the rowelling
of the cloth, the contours of his pitted skin,
I want to wash him, the way I would scrub
my dolls' faces thoroughly
before any great ceremony.

The Transformed One

When I was a child, the planes of his cheeks
were long and smooth, his brow pale ochre,
shaped like the bottom of a bowl, you could have
laid your hand on its curve like a god
setting a palm on the earth.
The slickour of his hair was like a joke on the goodness of his
        beauty—
in the evening he would not speak, or let us
speak, he would lie there, eyes closed,
sometimes making liquid garglings.
When I come to his hospital doorway in the morning
and see, around the curtain, the motionless
bulge of his feet, under the sheet,
I stop breathing. I walk in,
the starved shape of his body rises
and falls, and I breathe again,
I sit and breathe with him, tasting
the air as if we were in a greenhouse—
broken clay, the grave, wild mint,
dust-mite dust—or somewhere on the outskirts
of the garden of Eden, I do not know
which side of her hem we lie on, my unconscious
father and I.

Last Words

Three days ago, my suitcases
were hunched there, in his hospital room,
in the corner, I had to pick them up
by the scruff of their necks, and leave him. I kept
putting them down, and going back
to kiss him again although he was exhausted,
shining like tarnished silver, and yet
I could not seem to pick up those bags
and walk out the door the last time. I kept
going back to the mouth he would lift, his
forehead glittering with effort, his eyes
slewing back, shying, until
finally he cried out *Last kiss!*
and I kissed him and left. This morning, his wife
called to tell me he has ceased to speak,
so those are his last words to me,
the ones he is leaving me with—and it is ending with a *kiss—*
a command for mercy, the offer of his cracked
creator lips. To plead that I leave,
my father asked me for a kiss! I would not
leave till he had done so, I will not let thee go except thou beg for it.

Close to Death

Always, now, I feel it, a steady
even pressure, all over my body,
as if I were held in a flower-press.
I am waiting for the phone to ring,
they will say it and I will not be ready,
I do not have a place prepared,
I do not know what will happen to him
or where he will go. I always thought
I had a salvation for him, hidden,
even from myself, in my chest. But when the phone rings,
I don't know who he will be, then,
or where, I have nothing for him, no net,
no heaven to catch him—he taught me only
the earth, night, sleep, the male
body in its beauty and fearsomeness,
he set up that landscape for me
to go to him in, and I will go to him
and give to him, what he gave me I will give him,
the earth, night, sleep, beauty, fear.

Wonder

When she calls to tell me my father is dying
today or tomorrow, I walk down the hall
and feel that my mouth has fallen open
and my eyes are staring. The planet of his head
swam above my crib, I did not understand it.
His body came toward me in the lake over the agates,
the hair of his chest lifting like root-hairs—
I saw it and I did not understand it.
He lay, behind bevelled-glass doors, beside
the cut crystal decanter, its future
shards in upright bound sheaves.
He sat by his pool, not meeting our eyes,
his irises made of some boiled-down, viscous
satiny matter, undiscovered.
When he sickened, he began to turn to us,
when he sank down, he shined. I lowered my
mouth to the glistening tureen of his face
and he tilted himself toward me, a dazzling
meteor dropping down into the crib,
and now he is going to die. I walk down the
hall face to face with it
as if it were a great heat.
I feel like one of the shepherd children
when the star came down onto the roof.
But I am used to it, I stand in familiar
astonishment. I would have traded
places with anyone raised on love,
but how would anyone raised on love
bear this death?

The Race

When I got to the airport I rushed up to the desk,
bought a ticket, ten minutes later
they told me the flight was cancelled, the doctors
had said my father would not live through the night
and the flight was cancelled. A young man
with a dark blond moustache told me
another airline had a non-stop
leaving in seven minutes. See that
elevator over there, well go
down to the first floor, make a right, you'll
see a yellow bus, get off at the
second Pan Am terminal, I
ran, I who have no sense of direction
raced exactly where he'd told me, a fish
slipping upstream deftly against
the flow of the river. I jumped off that bus with those
bags I had thrown everything into
in five minutes, and ran, the bags
wagged me from side to side as if
to prove I was under the claims of the material,
I ran up to a man with a white flower on his breast,
I who always go to the end of the line, I said
Help me. He looked at my ticket, he said
Make a left and then a right, go up the moving stairs and then
run. I lumbered up the moving stairs,
at the top I saw the corridor,
and then I took a deep breath, I said
Goodbye to my body, goodbye to comfort,
I used my legs and heart as if I would
gladly use them up for this,
to touch him again in this life. I ran, and the

bags banged me, wheeled and coursed
in skewed orbits, I have seen pictures of
women running, their belongings tied
in scarves grasped in their fists, I blessed my
long legs he gave me, my strong
heart I abandoned to its own purpose,
I ran to Gate 17 and they were
just lifting the thick white
lozenge of the door to fit it into
the socket of the plane. Like the one who is not
too rich, I turned sideways and
slipped through the needle's eye, and then
I walked down the aisle toward my father. The jet
was full, and people's hair was shining, they were
smiling, the interior of the plane was filled with a
mist of gold endorphin light,
I wept as people weep when they enter heaven,
in massive relief. We lifted up
gently from one tip of the continent
and did not stop until we set down lightly on the
other edge, I walked into his room
and watched his chest rise slowly
and sink again, all night
I watched him breathe.

The Request

He lay like someone fallen from a high
place, only his eyes could swivel,
he cried out, we could hardly hear him,
we bent low, over him,
his wife and I, inches from his face,
trying to drink sip up breathe in
the sounds from his mouth. He lay with unseeing
open eyes, the fluid stood
in the back of his throat, and the voice was from there,
guttural, through unmoving lips, we could
not understand one word, he was down
so deep inside himself, we went closer, as if
leaning over the side of a well
and putting our heads down inside it. Once,
when his wife was across the room, he started to
gargle some of those physical sounds,
Rass - ih - AA, rass - ih - AA, I
hovered even lower, over his open
mouth, *Rass - ih - BAA,* I sank almost
into that body where my life half-began,
Frass - ih - BAA—"Frances back!"
I said, and he closed his eyes in his last
yes of exhausted acquiescence,
I said, She's here. She came over to him,
touched him, spoke to him, and he closed his
eyes, and he passed out and never
came up again, now he could move
steadily down.

Psalm

A lot of the time I just sat and held his foot.
The minister came, putting on his violet
stole, looping it over his head
as he walked in, an athlete binding
his wrist without thinking while approaching his event,
he read a Psalm, no longer going
close to my father and reading it next
to his ear, as he had when my father could still
turn his obedient unbeseeching
eyes toward a voice. You could see he was
beyond all that, *The Lord himself is thy keeper,*
the Lord is thy defense upon thy right hand, etc., etc.,
So that the sun shall not burn thee by day,
neither the moon by night. But my father would
stick his elbow out the window of his car, he
welcomed that L of fire on his elbow,
kiss of the god of long-distance drivers.
And he did not fear the heat of the moon, he would·
go to the edge of the pool any night
with a cigar, turning it, watching its fibrous
woven fire. Who knows what he was thinking,
or if he thought,
but he felt at ease with the moon and the sun
and his favorite table at each of his favorite
restaurants. So don't tell me
he need not fear, as if, now,
death would protect him, *The Lord shall preserve*
thy going out, and thy coming in,
from this time forth forevermore,
Amen, Goddamnit. I sat down
and held his foot again, cold

foot of the nearly dead—his feet that had
walked with the weight of me slung on his shoulder,
I breathed small breaths on them, and between each
puff I said my own psalm,
There is no good in this, there is
no good in this. And yet I had never
held his feet before, we had hardly
touched since the nights he had walked the floor at my arrival.

My Father's Eyes

The day before my father died
he lay there all day with his eyes open,
staring with a weary dogged look.
His irises had turned hazel in places
as if his nature had changed, bits
of water or sky set into his mineral solids.
Every time he blinked, the powerful
wave of the blink moved through my body
as if God had blinked,
a world unmade in the jump of an eyelid.
They said he was probably not seeing anything,
the material sphere of his eye simply
open to the stuff of the world.
But toward evening he would seem to move
his eyes toward my voice or his wife's voice.
And once, when he got agitated,
reaching out, I leaned down
and he swerved his blurred iris toward me and with-
in it for a moment his pupil narrowed and
took me in, it was my father
looking at me. This lasted just
a second, like the sudden flash
of sex that jumps between two people.
Then his vision sank back down
and left only the globe of the eye, and the
next day the soul went out
and left just my father there
and I thought of that last glint, glint without
warmth or hope, his glint of recognition.

The Last Day

The last day of my father's life
they bathed him in the morning, they drew the sheet down to his
        waist
and I sat with them and they washed him, clavicle,
shoulder, chest, ribs, the grainy
ochre skin, I looked out the window at the
folded California mountain,
I thought of how it was made when it was soft,
hot, malleable, I thought of my father
tiny and almost liquid inside his mother.
They soaped the angles of his body, I looked
at the mountain, at its crevices,
its areas of shadow and areas of light—
I have always longed to believe in what I am seeing.
They rolled the sheet up to his hips,
his thigh was just the femur now,
the skin like butcher paper wrapping
a bone for a dog, I saw the long
curve and the powerful knobs at the ends.
They dried him and the hair on his chest stood up,
they left the room a moment and I was
alone with him,
his nipple like a little handful of pebbles,
they brought the clean oven-heated
cotton cover and they turned his face to the window.
The daylight was shining into his mouth,
I could see a flake, upright, a limbless
figure, on his tongue, shudder with each
breath. The sides of his tongue were dotted with
ovals of mucus like discs of soft ivory,
I sat and gazed into his mouth, I had

never understood and I did not
understand it now, the body and the spirit.
Toward evening his breathing became more shallow,
the fog came in blue and powerful
over the houses and the redwoods,
I laid my head on the bed in the path of his breath and breathed it,
it was still sweet with its old soiled sweetness
the way dirt smells sour and clean.
An hour before he died he started to darken,
his breathing would stop for a few seconds
and start. His body began to bend,
turning away from the window, his skin was
a glassy yellow, he breathed and stopped
and breathed. I ran my hand through his hair
and kissed the side of his parched mouth. He took a breath,
and his wife and I stayed bent and waited
for the next breath. He was turned toward me,
his jaw open and his hair flowing back
like a man standing in a high wind, we
waited and waited for the next breath.
Then the nurse lifted his eyelids, and
in the white, under each iris,
a dark line had appeared. The nurse
pulled up his gown, I looked at the gentle
greyish slack stomach, the hair all
over it like a promise of animal kindness,
she laid the stethoscope against his heart
and waited, and then lowered the gown
and stepped back, and looked at me, and nodded,
and then I saw my father,
his emaciated head, his spine arched
as if to lift him away from the earth.
I put my head on the bed beside him
and breathed and he did not breathe, I breathed and
breathed and he darkened and lay there,
my father. I laid my hand on his chest

and I looked at him, at his eyelashes
and the pores of his skin, cracks in his lips,
dark rose-red inside the mouth,
springing hair deep in his nose, I
moved his head to set it straight on the pillow,
it moved so easily, and his ear,
gently crushed for the last hour,
unfolded in the air.

The Exact Moment of His Death

When he breathed his last breath, it was he,
my father, although he was so transformed
no one who had not been with him
for the last hour would know him—the skin
now physical as animal fat,
the eyes cast halfway back into his head,
the nose thinned, the mouth racked open,
with that tongue in it like the fact of the mortal,
a tongue so dried, scalloped, darkened
and material. We could see the fluid
risen into the back of his mouth
but it was he, the huge, slack arms,
the spots of blood under the skin
black and precise, we had come this far with him
step by step, it was he, his last
breath was his, not taken with desire
but his, light as a milkweed seed,
coming out of his mouth and floating across the room.
And when the nurse listened for his heart,
and his stomach was silvery, it was his stomach,
when she did not shake her head but stood and
nodded at me, for a moment it was fully
he, my father, dead but completely
himself, a man with an open mouth and
black spots on his arms. He looked like
someone killed in a bloodless struggle—
the strain in his neck and the base of his head,
as if he were violently pulling back.
He seemed to be holding still, then the skin
tightened slightly around his whole body
as if the purely physical were claiming him,

and then it was not my father,
it was not a man, it was not an animal,
I ran my hand slowly through the hair,
lifted my fingers up through the grey
waves of it, the unliving glistening
matter of this world.

His Smell

In the last days of my father's life
I tried to name his smell—like yeast,
ochre catalyst feeding in liquid,
eating malt, excreting mash—
sour ferment, intoxicant, exaltant, the
strong drink of my father's sweat,
I bent down over the hospital bed
and smelled it. It smelled like wet cement,
a sidewalk of crushed granite, quartz
and Jurassic shale, or the sour odor
of the hammered copper humidor
full of moist, bent, blackish
shreds of pipe tobacco; or the smelling-salts
tang of chlorine on the concrete floor of the
changing room at the pool in summer;
or the faint mold from the rug in his house
or the clouded pungence of the mouth and sputum
of a drinking man. And it was also the socket
of a man's leather shoe, acid with
polish and basic with stale socks—
always, in his smell, the sense
of stain and the attraction of the stain,
the harmony of oil and metal,
as if the life of manufacture and
industry were using his body
as a gland for their sweat. On the last day,
it rose on his forehead, a compound disc
of sweat, I brought it off on my lips.
After his last breath, he lay there
tilted on his side, not moving,

not breathing, making no sound,
but he smelled the same, that fresh tainted
industrial domestic male smell,
dark, reflecting points of light.
I had thought the last thing between us
would be a word, a look, a pressure
of touch, not that he would be dead
and I would be bending over him
smelling him, breathing him in
as you would breathe the air, deeply, before going into exile.

The Dead Body

I hated it, after he died, that we would sometimes
leave him alone in the room. For months there had
been someone with him, whether he was asleep
or awake, in coma, someone, and now
we would stand outside the door and he was
alone—as if all we had cared about was his consciousness,
this man who had so little consciousness, who was
90% his body. I hated
the way we were treating him like garbage, we would burn him, as if
only the soul mattered. Who *was* that,
if not he, lying there dried and abandoned.
I was ready to fight anybody
who did not treat that body with respect, just
let some medical students make a joke about his liver, I would
deck them, I so wanted to have someone to deck,
and if we were going to burn him, then
I wanted this man
burned whole, don't
let me see that arm on anyone in
Redwood City tomorrow, don't take that
tongue in transplant or that unwilling eye.
So what if his soul was gone, I knew him
soulless all my childhood, saw him
lying on the couch in the unlit end of the
living room on his back with his mouth open
and nothing there but his body. So I stood by him
in the hospital and stroked him, touched his
arm, his hair, I did not think he was there
but this was the one I had known anyway,
this man made of rich substance,

this raw one, like those early beings who
already lived on this earth before God
took that special clay and made his own set of people.

Death

Last night I saw James Cagney die
as Lon Chaney, he spelled out *I love you*
with his hands. His eyes were wry, narrowed,
as if savoring a cigar and a brandy, he spelled out
Forgive me with that keen savoring look,
then his head fell to the side. My father
was a reptile lifting its skull, his shoulders
rose up steadily, he was a lizard
approaching an insect,
his mouth was open as if he were pursued,
his hair sluicing back in motionless action.
When the hero dies, they draw away,
as if the dead need more space—
I was bent above my father as he curved up,
and when he died I wanted him to rise up
into me or me to climb down
into his body, we were like two baskets
ripped at the sides which could now be woven together.
He lay there, a child barely conceived
lying on the floor of heaven in a heap
with no one to go to. He darkened, then,
as if the room were getting brighter,
the way the lights come up at the end and you
look around—surely this
is not the world—

The Feelings

When the intern listened to the stopped heart
I stared at him, as if he or I
were wild, were from some other world, I had
lost the language of gestures, I could not
know what it meant for a stranger to push
the gown up along the body of my father.
My face was wet, my father's face
was faintly moist with the sweat of his life,
the last moments of hard work.
I was leaning against the wall, in the corner, and
he lay on the bed, we were both doing something,
and everyone else in the room believed in the Christian God,
they called my father *the shell on the bed,* I was the
only one there who knew
he was entirely gone, the only one
there to say goodbye to his body
that was all he was, I held hard
to his foot, I thought of the Eskimo elder
holding the stern of the death canoe, I
let him out slowly into the physical world.
I felt the dryness of his lips under
my lips, I felt how even my light
kiss moved his head on the pillow
the way things move as if on their own in shallow water,
I felt his hair rush through my fingers
like a wolf's, the walls shifted, the floor, the
ceiling wheeled as if I was not
walking out of the room but the room was
backing away around me. I would have
liked to stay beside him, ride by his

shoulder while they drove him to the place where they would
      burn him,
see him safely into the fire,
touch his ashes in their warmth, and bring my
finger to my tongue. The next morning,
I felt my husband's body on me
crushing me sweetly like a weight laid heavy on some
soft thing, some fruit, holding me
hard to this world. Yes the tears came
out like juice and sugar from the fruit—
the skin thins and breaks and rips, there are
laws on this earth and we live by them.

After Death

The last thing, in the hospital,
was leaving my father's wife alone
in the room with him. The death was done,
small, frail, last breath
had appeared from his mouth,
and she had spoken, fierce orator,
from the foot of his bed. I had left them a moment
and stood in the corner, pressing my forehead
into the right angle, the minister
had come, in his death stole, the disc of the
stethoscope had been slid back into
the intern's pocket, the women had sat
on either side and rubbed an arm,
a left arm and a right, there was one for each.
And the one on the bed lay, gaunt,
longed-for as he had always been,
and now not feared. Then we all left,
minister, doctor, nurse, daughter,
and his wife stayed, and the door closed.
Now was the center of the end. We stood
in the hall, apart, guarding the entrance,
silent, as if God were in there
unmaking a world. My mind was empty—
only weeks later, did I wonder
Did she lie on him, I think not, so
breakable. Did she kneel by the bed,
holding his hand, did she draw off the sheet
and look at him, a last time,
kiss his nipples, navel, dead
warm penis. The man himself
was safe, this was what he had sloughed.

It lay between them like a child of their love.
Did she draw the sheet back up to his chin,
cover you'd lay over a sleeping newborn,
eyes shut, mouth open
on a summer night—
she opened the door and came out, her wet
face shone, I had never seen her so calm.

What Shocked Me When My Father Died

Nothing shocked me about his death,
not that his face lost the rest of its flesh
as if his cheekbones were growing; not
the smallness of his last breath,
dust-ball under a doll-house bed; not the
open hearth of his mouth in death;
not his heart stopped, under
the hair. The fire that would burn him, the line
that appeared on his eyeball, the earth that would cover him—
nothing shocked me until I woke
beside my husband, and thought of how my father
did not struggle for air, how calmly
his body took its death, that final
tiny breath and then nothing, no effort—that
did not shock me but when I wept
and my husband laid his weight on me and the
tears covered my face hair ears as
if my head were underwater and I
sobbed and he quieted me—the children just
outside the door and my father's wife
through a thin wall—when he shushed my sobbing
by gently laying his palm over my
mouth almost as if thinking my sobbing
could sound as if I were coming, *that* shocked me.

Death and Murder

We tried to keep him alive, cut him and
piped him, tubed him, reamed him, practically
keelhauled him and it could not be done,
death took him, in our hands, and turned him
into that imitation of himself.
That's what murderers do, they take
your sight, taste, touch, hearing,
they set in your place the thing which looks
exactly like you, which can do nothing,
anything can be done to it
and it will not care, it is shameless, no honor
is innate to the body. When ordinary death
took my father, I did not understand
the act of murder, but I saw what murderers
do to you, they make you leave
and make you leave that doll of yourself behind you,
as if it were something the murderers had made,
 kneeling on the bank, scooping up the supple clay.

The Mortal One

All my life I had seen that long
glazed yellow narrow body,
not like Christ but like one of his saints,
or a hermit in gilt, all knees and raw ribs—
the ones who died of nettles, bile,
the one who died roasted over a fire.
I am glad we burned my father before
the bloom of mold could grow from him,
maybe it had begun in his bowels but we burned his bowels,
cleansing them with fire. Now I am learning
to think of his corpse without shock,
almost without grief, to take
the thought of it into each day, the way
when a loom parts the vertical threads,
half to the left half to the right, one can
throw the shuttlecock through with the warp-thread
tied to its feet, that small gold figure of my father—
how often I saw him in paintings and did not know him,
the tiny naked dead one in the corner,
the mortal one.

The Urn

I had thought it would be tapered, with a small
waist and a pair of handles, silver-
plated, like a loving cup
or tennis trophy, but there on the table
was a smooth, square box, with a military
look, the stainless steel corners
soldered up, a container that could bury
radium waste. I turned it till I turned
the name to me, that elegant label
like a name on a box of coarse salt—
this is who he was now, four or five
pounds of bone in a box, which I lifted
and rocked. There are people who swallow whole
cars, piece by piece, but the minister
was walking over, my stepmother approaching, I
held him and rocked him. I had not known
exactly where he was, or felt
the weight of him, since I had lifted up
his head by its warm nape to get the
fine tube of the oxygen harness
off his face after his death.
Now I had him back. I rubbed my
thumb over and over again
along the stainless steel. Whoever has
turned away from us, or could not
look at us, just the pressure of their weight feels like a blessing.

His Ashes

The urn was heavy, small but so heavy,
like the time, weeks before he died,
when he needed to stand, I got my shoulder
under his armpit, my cheek against his
naked freckled warm back
while she held the urinal for him—he had
lost half his body weight
and yet he was so heavy we could hardly hold him up
while he got the fluid out crackling and
sputtering like a wet fire. The urn
had that six-foot heaviness, it began
to warm in my hands as I held it, under
the blue fir tree, stroking it.
The shovel got the last earth
out of the grave—it must have made that
kind of gritty iron noise when they
scraped his ashes out of the grate—
the others would be here any minute and I
wanted to open the urn as if then
I would finally know him. On the wet lawn,
under the cones cloaked in their rosin, I
worked at the top, it gave and slipped off and
there it was, the actual matter of his being:
small, speckled lumps of bone
like eggs; a discolored curve of bone like a
fungus grown around a branch;
spotted pebbles—and the spots were the channels of his marrow
where the live orbs of the molecules
swam as if by their own strong will
and in each cell the chromosomes
tensed and flashed, tore themselves

away from themselves, leaving their shining
duplicates. I looked at the jumble
of shards like a crushed paper-wasp hive:
was that a bone of his wrist, was that from the
elegant knee he bent, was that
his jaw, was that from his skull that at birth was
flexible yet—I looked at him,
bone and the ash it lay in, silvery
white as the shimmering coils of dust
the earth leaves behind it as it rolls, you can
hear its heavy roaring as it rolls away.

Beyond Harm

A week after my father died
suddenly I understood
his fondness for me was safe—nothing
could touch it. In that last year,
his face would sometimes brighten when I would
enter the room, and his wife said
that once, when he was half asleep,
he smiled when she said my name. He respected
my spunk—when they tied me to the chair, that time,
they were tying up someone he respected, and when
he did not speak, for weeks, I was one of the
beings to whom he was not speaking,
someone with a place in his life. The last
week he even said it, once,
by mistake. I walked into his room and said
"How are you," and he said, "I love you
too." From then on, I had
that word to lose. Right up to the last
moment, I could make some mistake, offend him,
and with one of his old mouths of disgust he could
re-skew my life. I did not think of it much,
I was helping to take care of him,
wiping his face and watching him.
But then, a while after he died,
I suddenly thought, with amazement, he will always
love me now, and I laughed—he was dead, dead!

The Underlife

Waiting for the subway, looking down
into the pit where the train rides,
I see a section of grey rail de-
tach itself, and move along the packed
silt. It is the first rat I have seen
in years, at first I draw back, but then
I think of my son's mice and lean forward.
The rat is small, ash-grey,
silvery, filth-fluffy. You can see
light through the ears. It moves along the rail, it looks
cautious, domestic, innocent. Back
home, sitting on the bed, I see
an amber lozenge in the sheet's pattern
begin to move, and of course it's a cockroach,
it has lived in all the other great cities
before their razing and after it.
Christ you guys, I address these creatures,
I know about the plates of the earth shifting
over the liquid core, I watched the
bourbon and then the cancer pull my
father under, I know all this. And the
roach and rat turn to me
with that swivelling turn of natural animals, and they
say to me We are not educators,
we come to you from him.

One Year

When I got to his marker, I sat on it,
like sitting on the edge of someone's bed
and I rubbed the smooth, speckled granite.
I took some tears from my jaw and neck
and started to wash a corner of his stone.
Then a black and amber ant
ran out onto the granite, and off it,
and another ant hauled a dead
ant onto the stone, leaving it, and not coming back.
Ants ran down into the grooves of his name
and dates, down into the oval track of the
first name's O, middle name's O,
the short O of the last name,
and down into the hyphen between
his birth and death—little trough of his life.
Soft bugs appeared on my shoes,
like grains of pollen, I let them move on me,
I rinsed a dark fleck of mica,
and down inside the engraved letters
the first dots of lichen were appearing
like stars in early evening.
I saw the speedwell on the ground with its horns,
the coiled ferns, copper-beech blossoms, each
petal like that disc of matter which
swayed, on the last day, on his tongue.
Tamarack, Western hemlock,
manzanita, water birch
with its scored bark,
I put my arms around a trunk and squeezed it,
then I lay down on my father's grave.
The sun shone down on me, the powerful

ants walked on me. When I woke,
my cheek was crumbly, yellowish
with a mustard plaster of earth. Only
at the last minute did I think of his body
actually under me, the can of
bone, ash, soft as a goosedown
pillow that bursts in bed with the lovers.
When I kissed his stone it was not enough,
when I licked it my tongue went dry a moment, I
ate his dust, I tasted my dirt host.

The Swimmer

The way the seed that made me raced
ahead of the others, arms held to her sides,
round head humming, spine
whipping, I love to throw myself
into the sea—cold fresh
enormous palm around my scalp,
I open my eyes, and drift through the water that lies
heavy on the earth, I am suspended in it
like a sperm. Then I love to swim slowly,
I feel I am at the center of life, I am
inside God, there is sourweed in skeins like
blood beside my head. From the beach
you would see only the ocean, the swell
curling—so I am like a real being,
invisible, an amoeba that rides in spit,
I am like those elements my father turned into,
smoke, bone, salt. It is one of
the only things I like to do
anymore, get down inside the horizon
and feel what his new life is like, how
clean, how blank, how griefless, how without error—
the trance of matter.

The Exam

When I lie down to do a breast exam
I feel like my father in the hospital bed
about to take those last few breaths, I can feel myself in him,
my arms in his arms, my hands filling his hands,
my chest his chest—three breaths left,
lined up like a woman's last three eggs.
I don't know when he found the lump,
rising above his clavicle. But when I
lie down and get ready to die,
prepare to find a sphere hard as a
wizened pea-seed buried in my breast,
I can feel myself
slip into my father
wholly, deep inside his flesh
as if into a death-canoe
fitted tight to the body. He seemed
to love to point them out to me,
the humps, the stitches, the X-ray scorches, the
parchment map of his chest. When he left—
one, two, three, and then nothing—
he left the body on the bed like a cast
the cast-saw splits, they crack it open.
I wish I could say I saw a long
shapely leg pull free from the chrysalis, a
wet wing, a creature unfold and
fly out through the window, but he died down
into his body, sank and sank
until he was completely gone,
like a body buried in the earth and then dissolving.
I strip to the waist and lie spine-down
on the hardwood floor and walk walk walk my

fingers across my breast, explorers
out on the snowy pole, looking
for the tip of the axis. *Find nothing*,
my father hisses, and the fingers step step
step the way he used to do
the Itsy Bitsy Spider, slowly,
up my arm. His favorite part
was the sluice, the creature washed away,
and mine the return, the water-spout
dried off, the eight feet ascending,
the way it was endless.

Natural History

When I think about eels, I think about Seattle,
the day I went back to my father's grave.
I knew we had buried ashes, a box
of oily fluff, and yet, as I approached,
it felt as if the length of him
were slung there, massive, slack,
a six-foot amber eel flung down
deep into the hill. The air was clammy,
greenish as the old Aquarium air when we
would enter from the Zoo. Whenever we saw
a carnivore, my father would offer
to feed me to it—tigers, crocodiles,
manta rays, and that lone moray
eel, it would ripple up to us, armless,
legless, lipless as a grin of terror.
How would you like a tasty girl, my
father would ask the eel, a minister
performing a marriage, *How would you like
to get in there with that,* he'd lift me up the
thick glass, as if I were rising
on the power of my own scream. Later I would
pass the living room, and see him
asleep, passed out, undulant, lax,
indifferent. And at his grave
it was much like that—
the glossy stone, below it the mashed
bouquet of ashes, and under that,
like a boy who has thrown himself down to cry, the
great easy stopped curve
of my father. Length to length I lay on it
and slept.

The Cigars

I leaned on the glass case and gazed at them,
stiff scorched leaf of the earth,
some in aluminum tubes, some
in hinged cedar cases, most
loose in those papered balsa boxes.
One had swords and palm-fronds
on its lid, one had medals brown as
bruises—he had spots like that
from the X-ray beam, at his throat and neck.
Mottled leaf, smooth leaf,
soil-brown, raw umber,
cauled in cellophane—a display of
souls waiting to be conceived, or
brittle delicate penises, and
yet the man himself would wet them,
bite them, light them, as if tasting himself
in effigy. Always I would send one,
on birthdays, at Christmas, like a tribute, an annual tax,
a giving of the first fruits. And the cancer
came from smoking, and drinking. So I killed him—
the way he lay on the couch every night
he lay finally in the hospital bed
and then we burned him, his whole body
haloed in blue fire. And yet,
whenever I see a cigar, I have
an urge to give it to him. He loved
to peel the loud membrane off,
feel the springy little hand-rolled being,
nip the tip, hold the match
at the other end and suck. It was
his only song, that drawing in,

it was that song or none. And then,
for a moment, around his mouth, a cloud
blue as the white of a newborn's eye,
the soul he was born with.

Parent Visiting Day

In the science room, the model person
had been opened below the rib-cage—the plaster
liver lifted out and laid
aside, smooth, purple, a curved
ferric petal. The chest was shut,
both doors, the handles arched
like ichneumon wasps over the nipples.
Half the face was pulled from its slot,
the other half was looking down,
modest, fierce. No arms, no legs—
below the intestinal hole, where the hair
would curl, the figure ended in a swag
of pleated plaster drapery
as if the torso were standing in the grey Styx.
There was no one there to put their arms
around you after they were done with you
on the chrome gurney.
When I was a child, you lay, at night,
alive, a man who had removed his own
liver and brain and put them on the table, small
organ of the bourbon, large organ of the chaser.
If they had needed someone to descend
into you, to look for your soul,
swim the gluey river thick
with pieces of the dead—
if there had been a task to perform I would have performed it,
but you could not be helped. That was the point of hell.

Letter to My Father from 40,000 Feet

Dear Dad, I saw your double today
through the curtain to First Class. Reddish faced,
he had the pitted, swelled, fruit-sucker
skin cheeks lips of the alcoholic, still a
businessman, not fired yet.
He sat on the arm of his seat, chatting
across the aisle, I saw your salesman's
gaze, the eyes open and canny,
he had the shorn head, the loosened
tie, the shirt, the belt. I stared
through the split in the seats between us, and I wanted—
I wanted to go very close to him,
I did not want to gaze at him or kiss him,
I just wanted to put my long
arms around him, smell the ironed
cotton, feel the heat of his chest
against my cheek, the big male body
free of cancer, the fine sifted
lumpless batter of the flesh. Well, that's it, really,
just checking in. Isn't it something
the way I can't get over you, this
long, deep, unearned desire
you made when you made me, even after your death
it beams toward you, even when I'm dead I will be
facing you, my non-self
aiming this ardent non-love
steadily toward you. I guess I am saying
I hate you, too, there's a way I want
to take that first-class toper and throw him

down on the ground, arm-wrestle him
and win, bang his forearm on the earth
long after he cries out.

The Pull

As the flu goes on, I get thinner and thinner,
all winter, till my weight dips
to my college weight, and then drops below it,
drifts down through high school, and then
down into junior high,
down through the first blood,
heading for my childhood weight,
birth weight, conception. When I see myself naked
in the mirror, I see I am flirting with my father,
his cadaver the only body this thin
I have seen—I am walking around like his corpse
risen up and moving again, we
laugh about it a lot, my dead
dad and I. I do love being like him,
feeling my big joints slide
under the loose skin. My friends don't
think it's funny, this cake-walk
of the skeletons, and I can't explain it—
I wanted to lie down with him,
on the couch where he lay unconscious at night
and there on his death-bed, let myself down
beside him, and then, with my will, lift us both
up. Or maybe just lie with him
and never get up. Now that his dense
bones are in the ground, I am bringing
my body down. I'm not sure
how he felt about my life. Only twice
did he urge me to live—when the loop of his seed
roped me and drew me over into matter;
and once when I had the flu and he brought me
ten tiny Pyrex bowls

with ten leftovers down in the bottoms.
But when, in the last weeks of his life,
he let me feed him—slip the spoon
of heavy cream into his mouth
and pull it out through his closed lips,
I felt the suction of his tongue, his palate, his
head, his body, his death pulling at my hand.

The Ferryer

Three years after my father's death
he goes back to work. Unemployed
for twenty-five years, he's very glad
to be taken on again, shows up
on time, tireless worker. He sits
in the prow of the boat, sweet cox, turned
with his back to the carried. He is dead, but able
to kneel upright, facing forward
toward the other shore. Someone has closed
his mouth, so he looks more comfortable, not
thirsty or calling out, and his eyes
are open, there under the iris the black
line that appeared there in death. He is calm,
he is happy to be hired, he's in business again,
his new job is a joke between us and he
loves to have a joke with me, he keeps
a straight face. He waits, naked,
ivory bow figurehead,
ribs, nipples, lips, a gaunt
tall man, and when I bring people
and set them in the boat and push them off
my father poles them across the river
to the far bank. We don't speak,
he knows that this is simply someone
I want to get rid of, who makes me feel
ugly and afraid. I do not say
the way you did. He knows the labor
and loves it. When I dump someone in
he does not look back, he takes them straight
to hell. He wants to work for me
until I die. Then, he knows, I will

come to him, get in his boat
and be taken across, then hold out my broad
hand to his, help him ashore, we will
embrace like two who were never born,
naked, not breathing, then up to our chins we will
pull the dark blanket of earth and
rest together at the end of the working day.

The Motel

When I hear it's torn down I can hardly believe it,
I can see the square O of adobe
facing in, onto the inner
courtyard, and the pool, and the flowers, it feels
permanent as a Platonic idea,
as far beyond destruction as the Garden of Eden.
When I visited them I would stay there the last
night, next to the airport, get up
at six, put on my bathing suit
in the dark, open the glass and cross
the cold garden to the pool. Curls of
steam wandered up from the surface,
the birds in the palms awoke, I slid in
and sank and I was at home, in the green
breathless liquid world where I had often
gone with my father. The sicker he got,
those last months, the more I felt
this is where I would always find him—
underwater, body squeezed
in the water's airless hug.
I would pad back to my room, past
the bush with its stray camellia, the love
I longed for from him,
I'd turn on the hot, put my head under
as if it were upright Jordan, and I could
baptize myself his daughter, and now
it's a pile of rubbish—the tile surround,
palm-nuts, gardenia buds,
dirt, nests, girders. They will have
sold the beds, set aside the triple-milled
amber fluted soaps—and did they

save the pool, unsuction it up and
leave a hole like a grave, or did they
cave it in, Pompeiian. Anyway,
every trace of everything
that held me
holding him
will be removed from the planet. Only this small
oasis—sparrows and pittosporum,
a woman down inside the water, and
down inside her heart her snoring
father, and in his snore his daughter,
the pool, the courtyard, the city, the earth,
the universe, expanding blossom of wreckage.

I Wanted to Be There When My Father Died

I wanted to be there when my father died
because I wanted to see him die—
and not just to know him, down to
the ground, the dirt of his unmaking, and not
just to give him a last chance
to give me something, or take his loathing
back. All summer he had gagged, as if trying
to cough his whole esophagus out,
surely his pain and depression had appeased me,
and yet I wanted to see him die
not just to see no soul come
free of his body, no mucal genie of
spirit jump
forth from his mouth,
proving the body on earth is all we have got,
I wanted to watch my father die
because I hated him. Oh, I loved him,
my hands cherished him, laying him out,
but I had feared him so, his lying as if dead on the
flowered couch had pummelled me,
his silence had mauled me, I was an Eve
he took and pressed back into clay,
casual thumbs undoing the cheekbone
eyesocket rib pelvis ankle of the child
and now I watched him be undone and
someone in me gloried in it,
someone lying where he'd lain in chintz
Eden, some corpse girl, corkscrewed like
one of his amber spit-ems, smiled.
The priest was well called to that room,
violet grosgrain river of his ribbon laid

down well on that bank of flesh
where the daughter of death was made, it was well to say
Into other hands than ours
we commend this spirit.

When the Dead Ask My Father about Me

No, I could not speak about her.
This dirt, I have always had it in my mouth.
Now I carry it on my tongue, an honor—
a spoonful of the earth. But then my mouth
was grouted shut with its dark grout.
And I had her with a woman I did not love,
who did not love me. So I was glad it was
a second daughter, the way that woman
wanted a boy. And I liked the dark
curls like a beckoning hand palm up
on her scalp. I liked her sturdy curving
body, like my side of the family,
I liked her exaggerated passions, I loved
to pick up the foot of her bed, while she slept,
and drop it.
She was a dream to tease, she never
got it, she believed everything.
And I liked that she was bad, I would think of her
sitting there in the Principal's Office
where I had sat. I loved that she was never
hard on me, I walked from room
to room, carrying the soil in my mouth,
she never stopped me. She would stand in the doorway
to the living room, at night, when the dirt
was packed inside me and packed around me
on that six-foot couch—one snore-straw, from my nostril, sticking
up through it—I would sense her silently
hovering there, she was a little
afraid of me, she was a smart girl.
I was only in New York City once, in the
smallest room at the Waldorf, above

the furnace room—100 degrees—
I lived on Nabs. And when she moved to New York
she went to the Mayor's house for lunch, to
Gracie Mansion, on business. She could
speak, you see. As if my own
jaws, throat, and larynx had come
alive in her. But all she wanted
was that dirt from my tongue, umber lump you could
pass, mouth-to-mouth, she wanted us to
lie down, in a birth-room, and me
to labor it out, lever it into her
mouth I am audible, listen! this is *my* song.

To My Father

When I stood hip-deep in the pond, on a day
hushed with heat, and the maple creaked
and the catbird copied it, and I peed,
I looked down my naked body,
greenish with maple shade, and saw
the pee curl, oily and amber, in the
pewter spring-born water. Bourbon
down into icy crystal—I am with you,
sir, as if I have called you up
from the other world. Mysterious
as God, who are you? I think of you daily
but it isn't even you, a dead
man of ground bone, it wasn't
you even alive. You are not
the earth, or the seas, or the heavens, you are not
the air around us, or the bed, our loving
is not your being, we are not its two
lips. What have I worshipped?
I ask you this so seriously,
you who almost never spoke.
I have idolized the mouth of the silent man.
But now I have met you, coiling bourbon
genie of my urine, I have read the entrails
today, I have seen your gorgeous name
writ on water in waste, and pulled to the
dam and dashed down over it.

Waste Sonata

I think at some point I looked at my father
and thought *He's full of shit*. How did I
know fathers talked to their children,
kissed them? I knew. I saw him and judged him.
Whatever he poured into my mother
she hated, her face rippled like a thin
wing, sometimes, when she happened to be near him,
and the liquor he knocked into his body
felled him, slew the living tree,
loops of its grain started to cube,
petrify, coprofy, he was a
shit, but I felt he hated being a shit,
he had never imagined it could happen, this drunken
sleep was a spell laid on him—
by my mother! Well, I left to them
the passion of who did what to whom, it was a
baby in their bed they were rolling over on,
but I could not live with hating him.
I did not see that I had to. I stood
in that living room and saw him drowse
like the prince, in slobbrous beauty, I began
to think he was a kind of chalice,
a grail, his love the goal of a quest,
yes! He was the god of love
and I was a shit. I looked down at my forearm—
whatever was inside there
was not good, it was white stink,
bad manna. I looked in the mirror
and as I looked at my face the blemishes
arose, like pigs up out of the ground
to the witch's call. It was strange to me

that my body smelled sweet, it was proof I was
demonic, but at least I breathed out,
from the sour dazed scum within,
my father's truth. Well it's fun talking about this,
I love the terms of foulness. I have learned
to get pleasure from speaking of pain.
But to die, like this. To grow old and die
a child, lying to herself.
My father was not a shit. He was a man
failing at life. He had little shits
travelling through him while he lay there unconscious—
sometimes I don't let myself say
I loved him, anymore, but I feel
I almost love those shits that move through him,
shapely, those waste foetuses,
my mother, my sister, my brother, and me
in that purgatory.

My Father Speaks to Me from the Dead

I seem to have woken up in a pot-shed,
on clay, on shards, the bright paths
of slugs kiss-crossing my body. I don't know
where to start, with this grime on me.
I take the spider glue-net, plug
of the dead, out of my mouth, let's see
if where I have been I can do this.
I love your feet. I love your knees,
I love your our my legs, they are so
long because they are yours and mine
both. I love your—what can I call it,
between your legs, we never named it, the
glint and purity of its curls. I love
your rear end, I changed you once,
washed the detritus off your tiny
bottom, with my finger rubbed
the oil on you; when I touched your little
anus I crossed wires with God for a moment.
I never hated your shit—that was
your mother. I love your navel, thistle
seed fossil, even though
it's her print on you. Of course I love
your breasts—did you see me looking up
from within your daughter's face, as she nursed?
I love your bony shoulders and you know I
love your hair, thick and live
as earth. And I never hated your face,
I hated its eruptions. You know what I love?
I love your brain, its halves and silvery
folds, like a woman's labia.
I love in you

even what comes
from deep in your mother—your heart, that hard worker,
and your womb, it is a heaven to me,
I lie on its soft hills and gaze up
at its rosy vault.
I have been in a body without breath,
I have been in the morgue, in fire, in the slagged
chimney, in the air over the earth,
and buried in the earth, and pulled down
into the ocean—where I have been
I understand this life, I am matter,
your father, I made you, when I say now that I love you
I mean look down at your hand, move it,
that action is matter's love, for human
love go elsewhere.

Sharon Olds was born in 1942, in San Francisco, and educated at
Stanford University and Columbia University. Her first book of
poems, *Satan Says* (1980), received the inaugural San Francisco
Poetry Center Award. Her second, *The Dead and the Living*,
was both the Lamont Poetry Selection for 1983 and winner of the
National Book Critics Circle Award. She teaches poetry
workshops in the Graduate Creative Writing Program
at New York University and in the N.Y.U. workshop program
at Goldwater Hospital on Roosevelt Island in New York.

A NOTE ON THE TYPE

This book was set on the Linotype in Janson, a recutting made direct from type cast from matrices long thought to have been made by the Dutchman Anton Janson, who was a practicing type founder in Leipzig during the years 1668–1687. However, it has been conclusively demonstrated that these types are actually the work of Nicholas Kis (1650–1702), a Hungarian, who most probably learned his trade from the master Dutch type founder Dirk Voskens. The type is an excellent example of the influential and sturdy Dutch types that prevailed in England up to the time William Caslon developed his own incomparable designs from them.

Composed by Heritage Printers, Inc., Charlotte, North Carolina

Printed and bound by Arcata-Halliday Lithographers, Inc., West Hanover, Massachusetts

Based on a design by Judith Henry